BL: 5.1
AR: 0.5

11-18

SPACE MYSTERIES

WHAT IS SPACE JUNK?

Gareth Stevens PUBLISHING

BY TODD SWATLING

Please visit our website, www.garethstevens.com. For a free color catalog of all our high-quality books, call toll free 1-800-542-2595 or fax 1-877-542-2596.

Library of Congress Cataloging-in-Publication Data

Names: Swatling, Todd, author.
Title: What is space junk? / Todd Swatling.
Description: New York : Gareth Stevens Publishing, [2019] | Series: Space mysteries | Includes bibliographical references and index.
Identifiers: LCCN 2017056014| ISBN 9781538219676 (library bound) | ISBN 9781538219690 (pbk.) |
ISBN 9781538219706 (6 pack)
Subjects: LCSH: Space debris--Juvenile literature. | Spacepollution--Juvenile literature.
Classification: LCC TL1499 .S93 2018 | DDC 363.12/41--dc23
LC record available at https://lccn.loc.gov/2017056014

First Edition

Published in 2019 by
Gareth Stevens Publishing
111 East 14th Street, Suite 349
New York, NY 10003

Designer: Katelyn E. Reynolds
Editor: Joan Stoltman

Photo credits: Cover, p. 1 DAVID DUCROS/SCIENCE PHOTO LIBRARY/Getty Images; cover, pp. 1, 3–32 (background texture) David M. Schrader/Shutterstock.com; pp. 3–32 (fun fact graphic) © iStockphoto.com/spxChrome; p. 5 (main) ESA/ID&Sense/ONiRiXEL, CC BY-SA 3.0 IGO; p. 5 (inset), p. 13 (inset), 15, 19, 26 NASA; p. 7 ESA, CC BY-SA 3.0 IGO; p. 9 NASA/JPLCaltech; p. 11 (top) Edmund.huber/Wikipedia.org; p. 11 (bottom) Stamp produced by the United States Post Office Department/Wikipedia.org; p. 13 (main) ESA/J. Mai, CC BY-SA 3.0 IGO; p. 14 Tentotwo/Wikipedia.org; p. 17 (top) ESA/NASA; p. 17 (bottom) NASA/Srbauer/Wikipedia.org; p. 21 ESA–S. Laagland; p. 23 Cliff (http://flickr.com/photos/28567825@N03)/Wikipedia.org; p. 25 (background) suns07butterfly/Shutterstock.com; p. 27 ESA–David Ducros, 2016; p. 29 Johan Swanepoel/Shutterstock.com.

Printed in the United States of America

CPSIA compliance information: Batch #CS18GS: For further information contact Gareth Stevens, New York, New York at 1-800-542-2595.

CONTENTS

Words in the glossary appear in **bold** type the first time they are used in the text.

WHAT'S SPACE JUNK?

Space exploration is one of humankind's most amazing accomplishments. But did you know this **exploration** is making a big mess up there? It's leaving behind tiny bits of rocket shells, whole **satellites**, and many, many other objects. All the non-working things humans have left in **orbit** around Earth is called space junk. And it's becoming a problem.

Since people began exploring space in the 1950s, there have been over 5,000 **launches**. These created more than 500,000 pieces of space junk!

OUT OF THIS WORLD!

In 2008, an astronaut dropped a bag of tools outside the International Space Station. People on Earth could see it with **binoculars**!

metal chunk formed from rocket fuel

Each dot in this picture is an object orbiting Earth. It's pretty messy out there! Space junk is sometimes called orbital debris (deh-BREE).

5

WHAT'S THE BIG DEAL?

When scientists are planning to launch a spacecraft, they have to find a path that avoids hitting space junk. With hundreds of thousands of pieces scattered all around Earth, you can imagine it's a hard job!

All these pieces of space junk are flying around Earth at speeds of up to 17,500 miles (28,000 km) per hour. Crashing into a flake of paint traveling that fast would feel like getting hit by a grizzly bear moving 60 miles (97 km) per hour!

OUT OF THIS WORLD!

Scientists keep track of about 23,000 pieces of space junk, but there are millions more too small to track!

WHERE IS ALL THIS JUNK?

Before scientists can plan a safe path for a launch, they need to know where the space junk will be. They track it using **telescopes** and **radar**.

Objects as small as a golf ball can be tracked in low Earth orbit, which is from 110 to 1,200 miles (180 to 2,000 km) above Earth. Objects in high Earth orbit—more than 22,235 miles (35,780 km) up—have to be over 3 feet (1 m) wide to track.

OUT OF THIS WORLD!

Satellites in high Earth orbit move about as fast as Earth spins, so they're always over the same point on Earth. This is called a geosynchronous (jee-oh-SIHN-kreh-nehs) orbit.

Huge **antennae** such as this one use radar to track space junk.

9

EARLY SPACE JUNK

Years ago, talking to someone across the ocean required long wires under the water. And **communication** didn't work if something happened to the wires. Scientists found another way using **radio waves**, but these could be interrupted by the sun's energy.

In the 1960s, scientists put millions of needle-sized wires in low Earth orbit to act as a giant space antenna. It was called Project West Ford. It aided traveling radio waves, but created a lot of space junk!

OUT OF THIS WORLD!

The wires of Project West Ford were supposed to fall back to Earth after a few years, but many are still up there!

This photo shows part of one of the satellites that carried the copper needles into space.

Dipole Dispenser and Dipole Canister
Westford Communications Satellite
Launched by the U.S. Army in 1958, the Westford satellite used a unique concept to test the new undertaking of satellite communications from space. Once in space, the dispenser (with its spring mechanism) pushed the canister, packed with thousands of tiny needles (dipoles), into orbit. The needles in the canister slowly separated and formed a ring around the Earth. Antennas on the ground bounced radio signals off the ring of needles to communicate.

Transferred from the National Museum of American History

A20040113000
A20040113001

Project West Ford needles next to a postal stamp

THE BIG SKY THEORY

For years, scientists didn't think much of leaving things in space like the West Ford needles. They thought space was so big that they'd never see their space junk again. This idea is called the big sky theory.

However, in the 1970s, scientists at NASA (National Aeronautics and Space Administration) began working on rules to stop space junk from building up. The rules covered what could be left in space and what couldn't. By 2008, most countries followed similar rules.

OUT OF THIS WORLD!

NASA's Orbital Debris Program Office is located in Johnson Space Center in Houston, Texas.

Johnson Space Center

The European Space Agency (ESA) tracks space
junk from its operations center in Germany.

13

THE NEW PLAN FOR OLD SATELLITES

When a satellite in low Earth orbit gets old, scientists use up its fuel to slow it. Then, it falls from orbit and burns up in the atmosphere, which is the mix of gases that surrounds the planet. It's aimed at an area of the Pacific Ocean in case any bits reach the surface. This area is called Spacecraft Cemetery!

Satellites in high Earth orbit are pushed farther away, so they aren't near active satellites. They're placed in a "graveyard orbit" about 22,400 miles (36,050 km) above Earth.

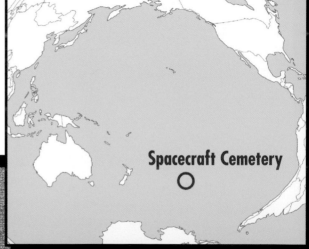

Spacecraft Cemetery

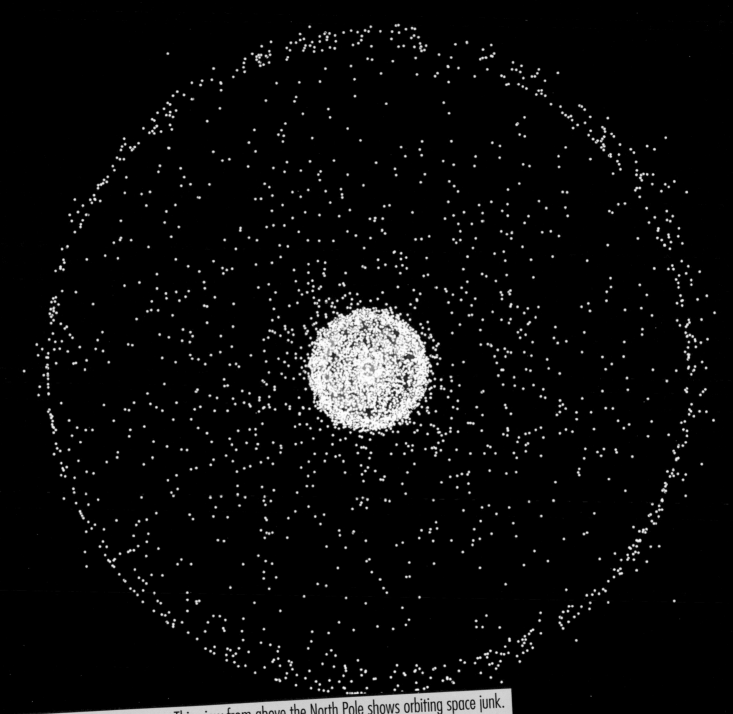

This view from above the North Pole shows orbiting space junk.
A graveyard orbit would be a little farther than the outer ring of space junk.

WHAT HAPPENS TO SPACE JUNK?

Gravity is always trying to pull orbiting objects down to Earth. When gravity finally pulls something into the atmosphere, **friction** heats it up. Space junk can get so hot that it burns up before reaching Earth. Objects larger than 4 inches (10 cm) don't completely burn, however. It's common for one to hit Earth every day!

Don't worry about getting smashed by space junk, though. Earth is mostly covered in water. So far, there have been no reports of people getting hurt by space junk.

OUT OF THIS WORLD!

When parts of NASA's Skylab space station crashed in Australia, the United States received a $400 fine for littering in the town of Esperance!

This is what it looks like when something burns up in Earth's atmosphere.

fuel tank from a spacecraft

17

HOW MUCH IS OUT THERE?

Since 1957, about 7,500 satellites have been launched into orbit around Earth. They're used for communication or scientific studies. There are about 4,300 satellites up there right now, but less than one-third are still working. The rest are space junk!

When two pieces of space junk crash into each other, they break apart. This creates thousands of new pieces of junk. Scientists think there have been over 290 of these kinds of space junk crashes so far. That explains why there's so much debris!

OUT OF THIS WORLD!

The combined weight of the man-made objects orbiting Earth is more than 8,200 tons (7,400 mt)!

Vanguard 1 is the oldest satellite that's still orbiting Earth. It's been up there since 1958!

19

A SATELLITE IN SHINING ARMOR

The best way for a spacecraft to deal with space junk is to avoid it. If that can't happen, the next best thing is for it to have a shield, or a covering that keeps it safe.

Many spacecraft use shields made of many layers of thin metal sheets. All those layers break up any space junk that hits the shield before it can hit the inner spacecraft. Sometimes there's also a blanket of tough cloth between the metal sheets.

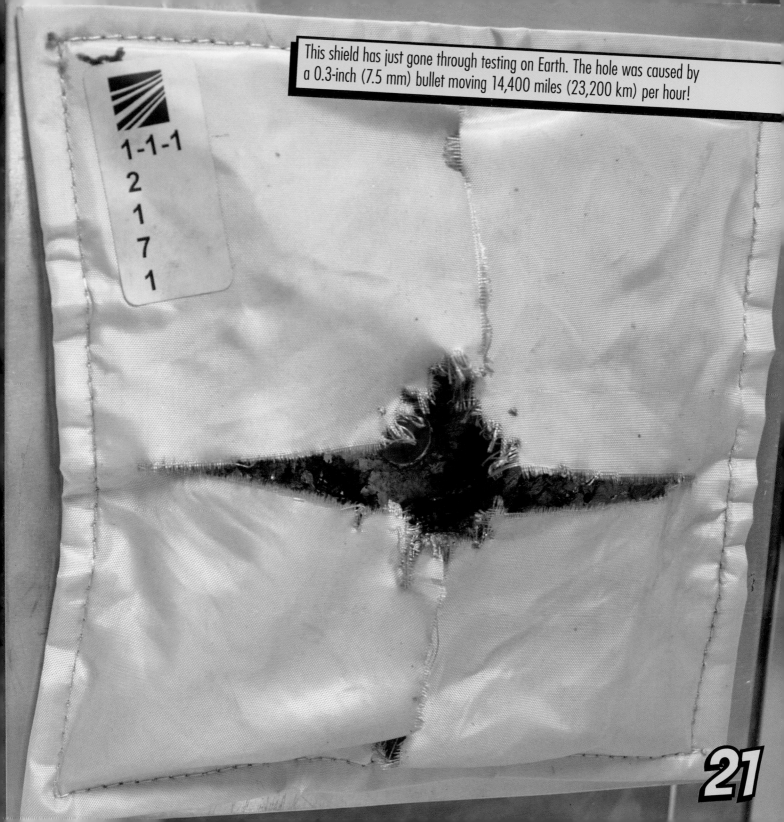

This shield has just gone through testing on Earth. The hole was caused by a 0.3-inch (7.5 mm) bullet moving 14,400 miles (23,200 km) per hour!

1-1-1
2
1
7
1

SMASHED SATELLITES

No amount of shielding could protect a satellite from what happened in 2009. Two satellites, Iridium 33 and Cosmos 2251, crashed into each other at about 26,000 miles (42,000 km) per hour! Before the crash, Iridium 33 was still working, but Cosmos 2251 had been shut down in 1995. It was the first time a working satellite was destroyed by another satellite by mistake.

After the crash, scientists found more than 3,200 new pieces of space junk. The pieces formed a ring around Earth that's still there!

Almost half the space junk from the crash of Iridium 33 (shown here) and Cosmos 2251 is still in space!

MORE DESTRUCTION

The Iridium 33 and Cosmos 2251 crash was an accident, but another satellite was blown up on purpose. In 2007, scientists in China wanted to test a way to destroy a satellite. A Chinese weather satellite called Fengyun-1C was chosen.

The test succeeded, and Fengyun-1C was destroyed. However, it created more than 2,600 pieces of space junk! Objects from this explosion are spread around low Earth orbit. This explosion holds the record for the most space junk produced from one event.

OUT OF THIS WORLD!

Some of the space junk from Fengyun-1C got very close to the International Space Station (ISS). At least once a year, the ISS has to move out of the way of approaching objects!

WHO PUT THE MOST JUNK IN SPACE?

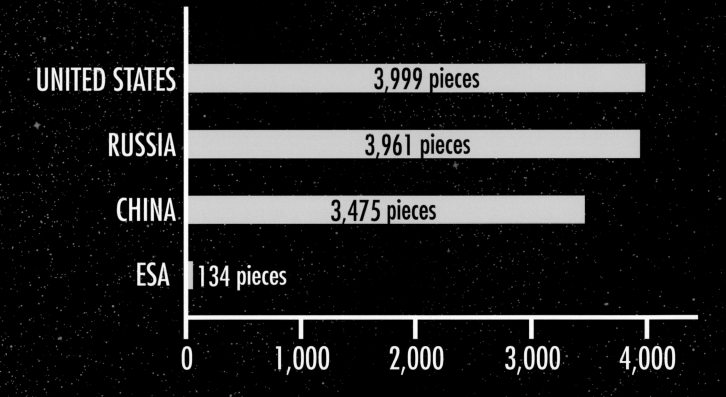

UNITED STATES	3,999 pieces
RUSSIA	3,961 pieces
CHINA	3,475 pieces
ESA	134 pieces

0   1,000   2,000   3,000   4,000

Because of Fengyun-1C, China is right behind the United States and Russia, the world's most space-polluting countries as of 2017.

CLEANING UP

Scientists have come up with ways to fix the space junk problem. One idea is to aim the sun's energy at pieces to burn them up. Another plan is to catch space junk with a net and pull it down.

Other scientists want to put a **laser** on the International Space Station so that it can shoot space junk that gets too close! None of these plans have happened yet because they cost a lot of money.

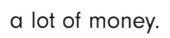

International Space Station

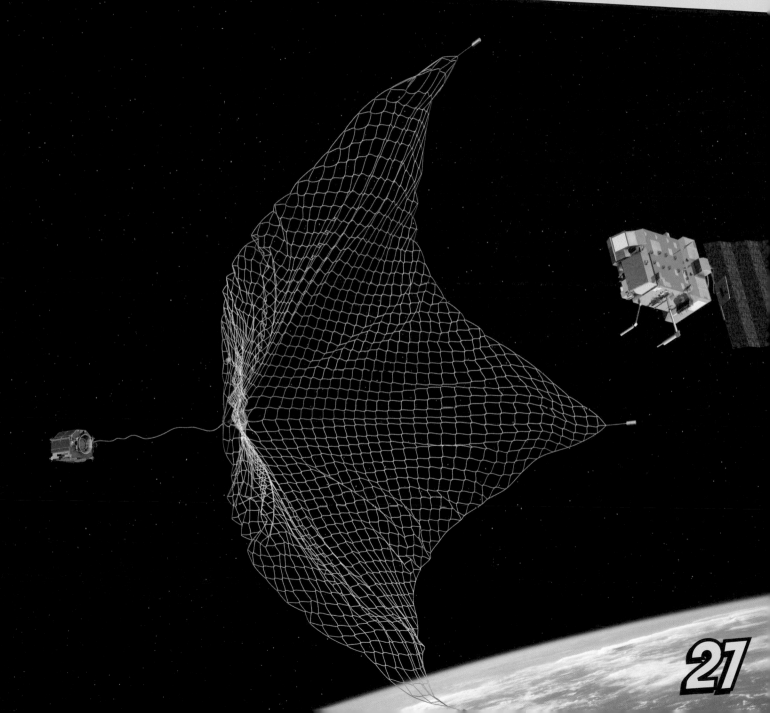

The European Space Agency is planning to launch the first cleanup spacecraft in 2023. It may use a robotic arm or a net, as pictured.

27

TOO MUCH CLUTTER

About 3,000 tons (2,700 mt) of space junk still remain in Earth's orbit. That's about the weight of 1,500 cars! If we don't start cleaning up, we might not be able to launch spacecraft or send important messages across the world by satellite. Space junk makes work in and around the International Space Station dangerous for astronauts, too.

The cleanup must begin soon. Will you be the scientist who invents the best way of cleaning up space?

OUT OF THIS WORLD!

NASA's Orbital Debris Program Office set a new goal. Twenty-five years after a satellite stops working, it should burn up in the atmosphere.

The future of space exploration is in danger because of space junk!

29

GLOSSARY

antenna: a metal rod or wire used to send and receive radio waves. The plural of "antenna" is "antennae."

binoculars: a tool that is held up to the eyes and looked through to see things that are far away

communication: sending information to people

exploration: the act of traveling through an unfamiliar place to learn more about it

friction: the force that slows motion between objects touching each other

gravity: the force that pulls objects toward Earth's center

laser: a tool that sends out a beam of light

launch: the sending of a rocket or spacecraft into the air with great force

orbit: to travel in a circle or oval around something, or the path used to make that trip

radar: a machine that uses radio waves to locate and identify objects. Also, a way of using radio waves to find distant objects.

radio wave: a wave of energy that is used for sending signals through the air without using wires

satellite: an object that circles Earth in order to collect and send information or aid in communication

telescope: a tool that makes faraway objects look bigger and closer

FOR MORE INFORMATION

BOOKS

Goldstein, Margaret J. *Garbage in Space: A Space Discovery Guide*. Minneapolis, MN: Lerner Publications, 2017.

Owen, Ruth. *Space Garbage*. New York, NY: PowerKids Press, 2015.

Silverman, Buffy. *Exploring Dangers in Space: Asteroids, Space Junk, and More*. Minneapolis, MN: Lerner Publications, 2012.

WEBSITES

Forecast for Reentry of Space Junk
www.satview.org/spacejunk.php
See when and where the next piece of space junk reenters Earth's atmosphere!

Stuff in Space
stuffin.space
See the paths of satellites and space junk around a spinning drawing of Earth.

INDEX